A GOVERNANCE FRAMEWORK FOR CLIMATE-RELEVANT PUBLIC INVESTMENT MANAGEMENT

FEBRUARY 2024

ASIAN DEVELOPMENT BANK

ADB

© 2024 Asian Development Bank
6 ADB Avenue, Mandaluyong City, 1550 Metro Manila, Philippines
Tel +63 2 8632 4444; Fax +63 2 8636 2444
www.adb.org

Some rights reserved. Published in 2024.

ISBN 978-92-9270-607-4 (print); 978-92-9270-608-1 (electronic); 978-92-9270-609-8 (ebook)
Publication Stock No. TCS240042
DOI: http://dx.doi.org/10.22617/TCS240042

Note:
In this publication, "$" refers to United States dollars.

Cover design by Maro de Guzman.

Contents

Tables, Figures, and Boxes

Foreword

Multilateral development banks are pivotal in aiding a greater and more sustained focus on climate-relevant public investment and public financial management by offering technical assistance and policy reforms to support green, inclusive, and resilient economic growth as well as leveraging their funds with private finance, and innovative and concessional funding mechanisms.

In 2022, the Asian Development Bank (ADB) committed $7.1 billion to climate finance, including $4.3 billion in climate change mitigation finance and $2.8 billion for climate change adaptation. ADB also mobilized $548 million in climate finance from the private sector. In addition, ADB shares knowledge solutions on emerging new technologies, practices, and policies that can accelerate the transitions to low-carbon and resilient economies.

This report provides a governance framework to address the urgent need for developing member countries to integrate adaptation and mitigation strategies into their public investment management (PIM) and public financial management (PFM) frameworks to close the climate investment gap. Good governance is crucial to deploying climate resources effectively and efficiently. Instead of establishing new institutions to fund or manage climate projects, governments should integrate climate considerations into PFM and PIM processes. Moreover, national climate plans should align with sector strategies and PFM and PIM processes for the consistent planning, funding, and implementation of projects.

Ministries of finance play a pivotal role. They should work with environmental and local agencies to ensure that fiscal strategies and budgets include climate funding. While public funds are essential, the private sector is vital as solution providers and financiers to bridge the investment gap and drive adaptation to climate risks. In projects requiring government support to be viable and reduce risks, the finance ministry or agency with similar functions must ensure the sustainability of budgetary funding needed throughout the project life cycle. Proper risk allocation between public and private sectors in public–private partnerships is also essential to incentivize private investors and can help to ensure a pipeline of viable climate-resilient projects. Robust governance of PFM and PIM processes is necessary to ensure that projects are gender- and climate-relevant and deliver tangible social and economic benefits while maintaining transparency and long-term sustainability.

Hiranya Mukhopadhyay
Director
Public Sector Management and Governance Sector Office
Sectors Group

About the Authors

Michael Schur, Infrastructure Finance Specialist

Schur has more than 25 years of global experience as an infrastructure finance and investment specialist and has chief executive experience in both the public and private sectors. He is currently an independent board member of a private concessions investment company and advisor to private and public sector clients, both in Australia and internationally. He has conducted risk assessments, project structuring, financial due diligence, and commercial negotiations on more than 25 privately financed infrastructure projects with a combined value of more than $30 billion in Australia, Cambodia, Ethiopia, India, Indonesia, New Zealand, the Philippines, South Africa, Uganda, and Viet Nam. He has a particular interest in infrastructure governance and in designing fiscal frameworks for managing infrastructure programs, whether delivered via public–private partnerships (PPPs) or by state-owned corporations.

David Bloomgarden, PPP and Public Investment Management Consultant

With more than 3 decades of experience in policy, management, and project design and implementation, Bloomgarden is an expert in public investment and PPPs. During his tenure as the chief of the Inclusive City Unit at the Inter-American Development Bank (IADB), he managed a $44.5 million project in Latin America and the Caribbean region overseeing the development of 40 blended finance investments for small and medium-sized enterprises in sustainable business models for urban services delivery. As the lead private sector specialist for PPPs, Bloomgarden spearheaded the IADB's Program to Promote PPPs in Latin America and the Caribbean, providing technical assistance to governments to enhance policy, project preparation, and implementation for sustainable infrastructure. He also created a PPP readiness index called "Infrascope," which was published by the Economist Intelligence Unit and used to assess PPP institutional capacity in Latin America and the Caribbean. After departing from the IADB, he worked as a PPP Specialist for the World Bank (Global Infrastructure Facility), the Asian Development Bank, and the European Bank for Reconstruction and Development, offering counsel on public investment management and quality infrastructure investment.

Abbreviations

ADB	Asian Development Bank
BAU	business as usual
COVID-19	coronavirus disease
DMC	developing member country
GDP	gross domestic product
GHG	greenhouse gas
IF-CAP	Innovative Finance Facility for Climate in Asia and the Pacific
NAP	national adaptation plan
NDC	nationally determined contribution
PIM	public investment management
PFM	public financial management
PPP	public–private partnership
SAI	Supreme Audit Institution
SDGs	Sustainable Development Goals
Sukuk	Islamic financial certificate, similar to a bond in Western finance, that complies with Islamic religious law commonly known as Sharia

Executive Summary

Significant infrastructure deficiencies exist—and climate change exacerbates these gaps—having dire implications for human welfare and economic growth. The interplay between investment shortfalls and those related to climate change creates a combined investment and climate gap. This report demonstrates that public financial management (PFM) and public investment management (PIM) processes play a crucial role in determining the quality of the preparation and implementation of climate-relevant investments needed to close this combined investment gap. Inefficient infrastructure governance is responsible for losing more than one-third of the impact of resources meant for public infrastructure. This report presents data and country examples to show that enhancing these governance processes can significantly improve the quality of investment and deployment of climate finance. At its heart, PFM revolves around the budget cycle, which has four primary steps: setting fiscal targets, budget preparation, budget execution, and audit and evaluation. A "green" PFM system aims to incorporate climate considerations into regular PFM processes. This method seeks to combine climate-relevant planning with the conventional four-step budget cycle, surrounded by a broader process of fiscal transparency.

PIM is a subset of PFM that oversees public investment planning, project evaluation, and the delivery of investments, including those targeting climate objectives. The PIM process consists of three main stages: investment planning, project appraisal, and project delivery. Strong governance in PIM is pivotal for bridging the investment and climate gap and ensuring optimal project selection, planning, and implementation. Several governance principles are vital for successful climate-relevant PIM processes, including institutional capacity, whole-of-government coordination, standardized evaluation criteria, transparency and accountability, stakeholder participation, independent scrutiny such as external audits, and consistency and predictability of rules and regulations to ensure fairness and clarity.

The report concludes that to tackle the challenges present in climate-relevant PIM and PFM processes, countries should integrate adaptation and mitigation strategies into their regular ("business as usual" or BAU) investment planning. This can be achieved by investing in a comprehensive understanding of climate change risks specific to sectors, adopting rolling investment plans for more flexibility, inclusive planning to include all stakeholders in the planning process, sound risk allocation and management, and establishing approval processes that include the technical capacity to review and understand the fiscal costs of climate risks. The divide in responsibilities between BAU investment planning (handled by line ministries) through the budget process and planning for nationally determined contributions under the Paris Accords and national adaptation planning (managed by centralized agencies)—often divorced from the budget process—

impedes coordination and often results in two distinct investment planning tracks: one for BAU and another for climate change mitigation and adaptation. Adaptation and mitigation plans—isolated from BAU budget processes—might not undergo the same rigorous planning, allocation, and implementation, and dedicated climate institutions might not be fiscally synchronized with PFM processes, creating disparities in funding allocation. In essence, countries need to develop and evaluate climate-relevant projects within the same best practice PIM and PFM frameworks as regular investments to ensure effectiveness and alignment with broader national objectives.

Introduction

The literature on climate change impacts is expanding and revealing more alarming projections, including extreme weather events and rising temperatures, sea levels, and water salinity. While the urgency to mitigate and adapt to climate change is widely accepted, investments in these areas remain insufficient. International consensus on the need for action has grown, as evidenced by the establishment of institutions like the Intergovernmental Panel on Climate Change and agreements such as the United Nations Framework Convention on Climate Change, Kyoto Protocol, Copenhagen Accord, and Paris Agreement. The Asian Development Bank (ADB) has prioritized combating climate change and its consequences, committing to provide $100 billion in climate financing from its own resources to developing member countries (DMCs) during 2019–2030. ADB supports policies, practices, and technologies that reduce greenhouse gas (GHG) emissions and integrate a comprehensive approach to climate and disaster resilience. ADB's work also emphasizes environmental sustainability and recognizes the interconnectedness of water, food, and energy.[1] In addition, ADB launched the Innovative Finance Facility for Climate in Asia and the Pacific (IF-CAP), a multi-donor facility that could unlock billions of dollars in climate change financing. Through a leveraging model of "one dollar in, five dollars out," the initial $3 billion in guarantees could create up to $15 billion in new loans for crucial climate initiatives in Asia and the Pacific.[2]

While emissions reduction targets under the Paris Agreement as of 2023 would lead to an 11.0% decrease in GHG emissions, substantial financing—trillions of dollars annually until 2050—is required to achieve this goal. However, the global deployment of climate finance only amounts to $630 billion per year (as of 2023), which does not take into account the substantial funding requirement for operations and maintenance to ensure the sustainability of infrastructure assets. As a result, inadequate mitigation efforts will escalate climate risks, and insufficient adaptation measures will lead to even greater losses and fiscal costs globally.[3] To bridge the investment gap, it is crucial to understand the underlying reasons for significant underinvestment thus far. This report examines the role of DMC governance in the investment gap and proposes a framework to integrate climate responses into governance frameworks, thereby supporting the scaling up of adaptation and mitigation investments. By drawing on governance experiences from other sectors, this analysis seeks to enhance governance approaches to climate change, considering the widespread nature of investment gaps.

---

[1] ADB. 2021. ADB Raises 2019–2030 Climate Finance Ambition to $100 Billion. News release. Manila.
[2] See IF-CAP: Innovative Finance Facility for Climate in Asia and the Pacific.
[3] B. Li. 2023. Scaling up Climate Finance for Emerging Markets and Developing Economies. Speech by Deputy Managing Director Bo Li at EIB Group Forum 2023. 27 February. Washington, DC: International Monetary Fund (IMF).

2 The Climate Investment Gap Is Widening the Existing Investment Gap

Significant infrastructure gaps exist before and outside of the specific dynamics of climate change. About 940 million individuals are without electricity, 663 million lack improved sources of drinking water, 2.4 billion lack improved sanitation facilities, 1 billion live more than 2 kilometers from an all-season road, and uncounted numbers are unable to access work and educational opportunities because of the absence or high cost of transport services.[4] Climate change causes additional impacts and risks and widens the investment gap with far-reaching consequences for human well-being and economic growth. Asia and the Pacific are facing more frequent and wide-ranging climate-related challenges than most other regions. More than 40.0% of global climate-related disasters have occurred in the region since the start of the 21st century, affecting nearly 3.6 billion people and causing almost 0.9 million deaths. Rising temperatures, increased frequency and intensity of extreme weather events, and rising sea levels are among the main climate-related triggers that threaten human and physical assets, especially since populations across Asia and the Pacific are concentrated in coastal and urban areas. DMCs have experienced physical losses worth billions of dollars because of climate-related events. In 2020 alone, the region faced a disaster loss of $67 billion. Estimates suggest that the increase in annual losses will outpace gross domestic product growth in Asia and the Pacific if left unaddressed.[5]

The size of the climate investment gap in terms of adaptation and mitigation varies by country, including its specific climate, topography, and the sector makeup of its economy. The largest climate investment gaps are found in Africa, Asia, and Latin America. In Asia and the Pacific, ADB estimates the region needs to invest about $26.2 trillion during 2016–2030 if countries are to restore economic growth momentum to pre-coronavirus disease (COVID-19) pandemic levels, eliminate poverty, and invest in climate-resilient infrastructure for water, communications, transport, and power.[6] The key climate risks by sector that drive the need for climate investment are summarized in Table 1.

---

4   J. Rozenberg and M. Fay. 2019. Beyond the Gap: How Countries Can Afford the Infrastructure They Need while Protecting the Planet. Sustainable Infrastructure. Washington, DC: World Bank.

5   ADB. 2023. Establishment of the Innovative Finance Facility for Climate in Asia and the Pacific Financing Partnership Facility. Internal report.

6   ADB. 2018. Strategy 2030: Achieving a Prosperous, Inclusive, Resilient, and Sustainable Asia and the Pacific. Data based on estimated Infrastructure Investment Needs by Sector, 2016–2030 (2015 prices).

Table 1: Key Infrastructure Climate Risks by Sector

Sector	Key Infrastructure Climate Risks
Energy	Increased frequency and intensity of extreme weather events
	Rising sea levels and coastal erosion
	Heatwaves and higher temperatures lead to increased energy demand
	Disruption of power generation and transmission
	Damages to power plants and renewable energy installations
Transportation	Increased flooding and storm damage to transportation networks
	Disruption of road, rail, and air travel because of extreme weather
	Damage to bridges, tunnels, and ports
	Increased risks to coastal transportation infrastructure
Water and Sanitation	Reduced water availability and increased drought risks
	Increased flooding and water contamination
	Damages to water treatment and distribution systems
	Risks to wastewater treatment and sewage systems
Buildings	Increased vulnerability to hurricanes and windstorms
	Higher risks of structural damage and collapse
	Increased energy consumption for cooling and heating
	Risks of flooding and water infiltration
Agriculture	Changing rainfall patterns and prolonged droughts
	Increased risks of crop failures and decreased yields
	Risks to irrigation systems and water storage facilities
	Increased vulnerability of farm buildings and infrastructure
Coastal	Rising sea levels and coastal erosion
	Increased risks of storm surge and coastal flooding
	Damage to coastal infrastructure and buildings
	Risks to ports, harbors, and coastal defenses

Source: Authors.

The forces of investment gaps and climate investment gaps are best understood together as a combined investment gap. With the added pressures of climate change, countries face even greater challenges to make progress toward the Sustainable Development Goals (SDGs). Combined, the World Bank[7] estimates the overall investment gap as about 4.5% of gross domestic product (GDP) for low- and

---

[7]   J. Rozenberg and M. Fay. 2019. *Beyond the Gap: How Countries Can Afford the Infrastructure They Need while Protecting the Planet.* Sustainable Infrastructure. Washington, DC: World Bank.

middle-income countries to achieve the infrastructure-related SDGs as well as to stay on track to limit climate change to 2°C.

The size of the combined climate and investment gap cannot be met by public resources alone and requires private investment in climate change mitigation and adaptation. However, only a small share of private climate finance goes to developing countries. The private sector funds 81.0% of green investment in high-income countries as of 2023, but only 14.0% in developing countries where financing costs can be up to seven times higher.[8] One of the reasons for the small share of climate finance in developing countries is the lack of investable projects and a conducive policy environment. Climate investment funds, for example, seek a steady flow of "bankable" investments that meet a range of evaluation criteria to determine whether finance can be granted. One of the largest dedicated green finance institutions— the Green Climate Fund—requires investments to demonstrate impact potential, paradigm shift, sustainable development, need of recipients, country ownership, and efficiency and effectiveness.[9]

---

[8]   H. Halland, J. Y. Lin, and A. Gelb. 2023. *What the Paris Development Finance Summit Missed.* Project Syndicate. 10 July.

[9]   For information on Green Climate Fund funding access, modalities, and programs, see https://www. greenclimate.fund/.

Toward Improved Governance for Climate-Informed Public Financial and Public Investment Management Processes

3

Greening Public Financial Management Processes

High quality public financial management (PFM) and public investment management (PIM) processes determine the quality of investment preparation and execution. Improving these processes and the governance within them is critical to improving the quality of investment propositions and unblocking the deployment of climate finance. On average, more than one-third of the resources spent on creating and maintaining public infrastructure are lost because of inefficiencies closely linked to governance.[10] Estimates suggest that, on average, better *infrastructure governance*[11] could make up more than half of the observed efficiency losses.[12] This research indicates that the most rapid improvement countries can make in closing the investment gap is through improved governance within PFM and PIM processes, rather than, for example, through expanding access to finance.

Public financial management refers to the set of laws, organizations, systems, and processes that governments employ to effectively manage their financial resources. PFM encompasses all activities related to budgeting, revenue collection, expenditure management, accounting, auditing, and reporting within the public sector. Green PFM refers to the institutional arrangements in place to facilitate the implementation of fiscal policies that support climate-sensitive policies.[13] PFM is "what makes fiscal policy work"[14]; it is about the institutional and practical arrangements that ensure that fiscal policies are optimally designed and implemented.[15] At the core of PFM is the budget cycle, which is the annual process by which governments formulate, approve, execute, and evaluate their budgets. The typical budget cycle is envisioned as a four-step cycle, anchored by a legal framework. The four steps are:

---

[10] G. Schwartz et al., eds. 2020. *Well Spent: How Strong Infrastructure Governance Can End Waste in Public Investment.* p. 1. Washington, DC: IMF.

[11] Infrastructure governance as used in this publication is defined as the institutions and frameworks for planning, allocating, and implementing infrastructure investment.

[12] G. Schwartz et al., eds. 2020. *Well Spent: How Strong Infrastructure Governance Can End Waste in Public Investment.* Chapter 3.

[13] The term "green" generally pertains to environmental sustainability and eco-friendly practices, and "climate" refers to the patterns and long-term changes in the earth's atmospheric conditions. The two concepts are intertwined in the context of addressing global climate change.

[14] R. Hemming. 2013. The Macroeconomic Framework for Managing Public Finances. In R. Allen, R. Hemming, and B. H. Potter, eds. *The International Handbook of Public Financial Management.* Palgrave Macmillan.

[15] Gonguet et al. 2021. *Climate-Sensitive Management of Public Finances—"Green PFM".* IMF Staff Climate Note 2021/002. Washington, DC: IMF.

(i) **Setting fiscal targets**. This stage refers to the setting of a framework for strategic and fiscal policy goals and targets in line with a medium-term fiscal framework.[16] The fiscal framework could be used to define medium-term fiscal targets that are consistent with the costing of green priorities such as the reduction of GHG emissions while ensuring fiscal discipline. Flexible fiscal rules are needed to allow for a fiscal response in case of a climate-change-related emergency. Fiscal rules could be accompanied by an escape clause that allows for their suspension in the wake of large disasters.

(ii) **Budget preparation**. Based on the medium-term fiscal framework and sector strategies, a finance ministry or similar agency prepares the annual budget for approval by a legislative body. The budget circular is an important document produced by budget departments that provides operational guidelines and targets to be shared with sector ministries before budget preparation. It is also an effective tool for incorporating environmental or climate-related instructions into budget decisions. Green budget tagging is a valuable tool that assesses each component of the budget based on its climate or environmental impact and gives it a "tag" according to whether it is helpful or harmful to green objectives. This helps to highlight the true importance of climate change concerns in resource allocation and monitor progress from 1 year to the other.

(iii) **Budget execution**. This stage refers to the execution of the approved budget and the production of accounts and financial reports. In this phase, reporting on climate-related expenditure is an important part of an effective green PFM system. Climate tagging can only reach its potential when used both for budget formulation and during budget execution. Tracking of green expenditure should ideally be factored in from the outset when putting a tagging system in place. Governments should ensure that the financial management information system has adequate functionality for accounting and reporting of climate-related expenditure. Some countries may also choose to rely on ad hoc reporting by line ministries to track actual green spending. The reporting should allow a direct comparison between budget and actuals.

(iv) **Audit and evaluation**. This stage includes independent oversight and audit of the budget and program evaluation. Control and audit mechanisms should examine, measure, and monitor the efficiency and effectiveness of climate policies. The finance ministry and line ministries and agencies perform the internal control and audit. The Supreme Audit Institution (SAI) performs the external audit. All stakeholders should control and evaluate the climate impact of government policies. Line ministries and agencies should monitor and assess the climate outputs attached to their budget actions. Internal audit or inspection bodies can also adopt a climate focus in their work program. State audit institutions could assess compliance of government programs or projects and transactions with climate-related objectives and requirements. Parliament could examine the reports of the SAI and related evaluation reports on climate strategies.

---

[16] A medium-term fiscal framework is a comprehensive description of fiscal policy objectives and goals based on macroeconomic projections. It is essential for sustainable budget preparation processes that go beyond the annual budget cycle.

An approach that integrates climate considerations into PFM processes can significantly improve governance. A "green" PFM process seeks to mainstream climate considerations and unify the institutions and frameworks addressing climate change with "business as usual" PIM and PFM processes. Figure 1—with the four-step budget cycle in the center—illustrates the integration with specific climate-related planning, execution, tracking, and review enclosed within the overall process of fiscal transparency. At each layer, climate considerations are integrated with the wider set of country strategies and plans. This approach aims to leverage PFM systems and tools of budgetary policymaking to achieve climate commitments and other green priorities while avoiding fragmentation of the core PFM and budget processes.

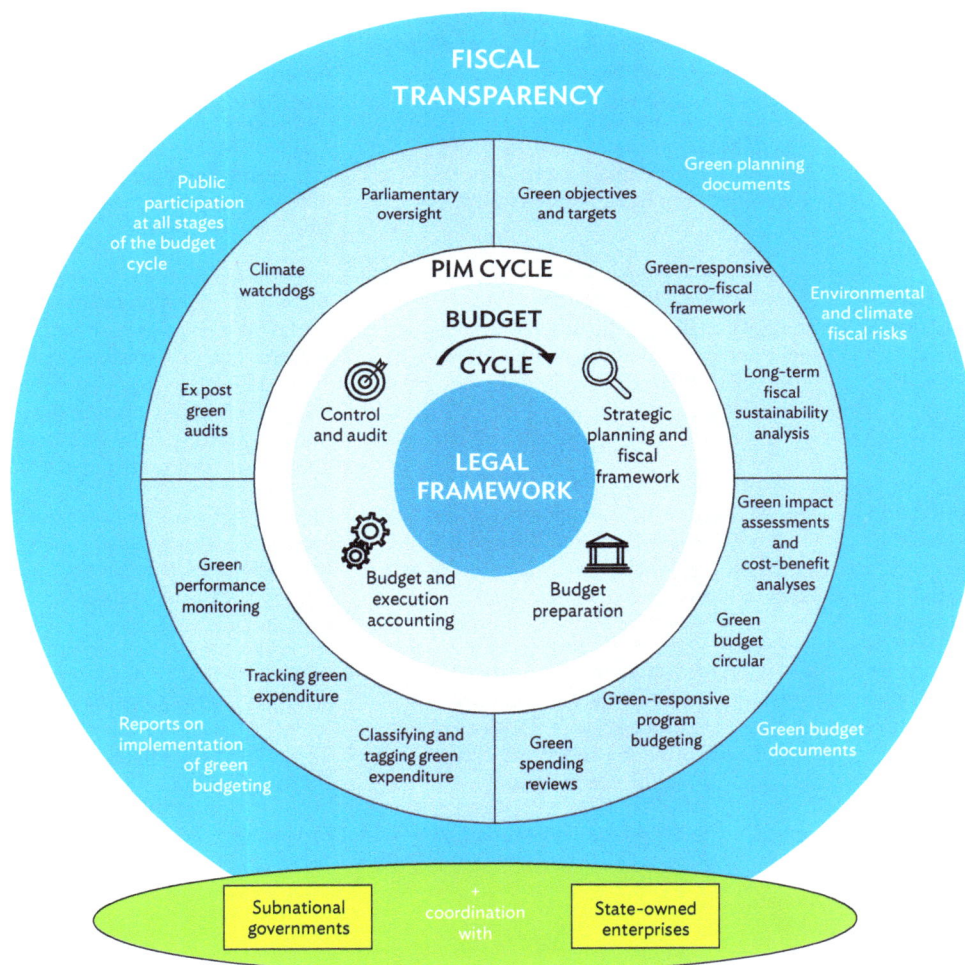

Figure 1: The Green Public Financial Management Process

PIM = public investment management.

Source: F. Gonguet et al. 2021. Climate-Sensitive Management of Public Finances—"Green PFM." IMF Staff Climate Note 2021/002. Washington, DC: International Monetary Fund.

Countries have implemented a range of approaches to improve the climate responsiveness of their PFM frameworks. While still in its nascent stage in many countries including advanced countries, progress is being made across a wide range of geographies and economies to integrate climate into the PFM framework. Table 2 summarizes a range of initiatives across the five components of PFM and country examples of where they have been implemented.

Table 2: Country Examples of Climate-Informed Public Financial Management Initiatives

Public Financial Management Component	Example	Example
Legal Framework—underpins the budget cycle and PFM practices	Dedicated climate change laws with mitigation and adaptation objectives, mechanisms to achieve and monitor, and assignment of institutional duties and powers to this effect: the Philippines, the United Kingdom, and Kenya	Inclusion of PFM elements in climate laws—linking climate change with the annual budget process: Sweden Amended public finance laws to integrate green practices: New Zealand and Mexico
Strategic Planning and Fiscal Framework—green priorities taken on board, within overall fiscal constraints	Macro fiscal forecasting and modeling incorporates climate impacts: Denmark's Green Reform project and Sweden's Climate Report	Flexible fiscal rules in case of a climate-change-related emergency, e.g., suspension in the wake of major disasters: Germany, Maldives, and Brazil
Budget Preparation—crucial phase for the inclusion of green priorities and concerns	Climate-related instructions in the budget circulars, justification of all new policy proposals in terms of their climate impact: Bangladesh, France, Pakistan, and Burkina Faso	Systematic inclusion of environmental and climate dimensions in impact assessments and cost–benefit analyses: Australia, France "Greening" of expenditure review processes – VFM and contribution to environmental and climate goals: Ireland
Budget Execution and Accounting—keeping track of and reporting on climate-related expenditure	Budget tagging to provide an overall picture of climate-related expenditure and tax expenditure: Bangladesh, France, Indonesia, Ireland, Nepal, and the Philippines	Preparing PFM systems for the challenges associated with emergency responses: the Philippines, the United Kingdom
Control and Audit—to examine, measure, and monitor the efficiency and effectiveness of climate policies	SAI assesses compliance of government programs and projects and transactions with climate-related objectives: Bangladesh's climate performance audit methodology, Canada (as part of existing audit)	Establishment of a dedicated independent body to oversee government climate initiatives: Ireland's Climate Change Advisory Council and the Philippines' Committee on Climate Change

PFM = public financial management, SAI = Supreme Audit Institution, VFM = value for money.

Source: F. Gonguet et al. 2021. Climate-Sensitive Management of Public Finances—"Green PFM." IMF Staff Climate Note 2021/002. Washington, DC: International Monetary Fund.

Greening Public Investment Management Processes

Within PFM, PIM processes control public investment planning; project appraisal and selection; and funding, financing, and delivery of investments including those with climate-related objectives. A green PIM refers to the strategic planning, allocation, and oversight of public funds toward projects and initiatives that aim to promote environmental sustainability and combat climate change. There are three key stages of public investment: (i) investment planning, which includes needs assessment, setting strategic objectives, and project identification and prioritization; (ii) project appraisal, which includes resource allocation, project evaluation, and selection for implementation; and (iii) funding, financing, and project delivery, which includes project management, structuring, procurement and contracting, quality control and monitoring, and asset management and maintenance.

The PIM cycle is integrated with the PFM budget cycle, with prioritized and prepared projects being assessed for resource allocation as part of the budget process. Once projects are fully funded and receive budget allocation, they can then be financed and implemented.[17] A focused PIM within a PFM should improve governance because PFM processes as a whole must be made more climate responsive. It is within PIM processes that a large proportion of climate spending will occur, including, for example, on renewable energy generation plants, climate-proofed infrastructure, and coastal resilience projects that support a range of solutions to help the coastal area adapt to accelerated sea level rise.

Strong governance within a PIM is critical to closing the investment gap. Since the institutions and frameworks constitute governance, strong governance ensures that projects are chosen using best-practice investment planning and prioritization processes and project appraisal processes. Projects are prioritized and funded to deliver the greatest benefits and sustainability within the country's fiscal strategy and funding and financing limitations. The projects are then implemented using best practice "green" procurement processes,[18] project execution, and operations monitoring processes.[19] Strong governance processes increase green public investment efficiency directly through deploying public resources in a staged way that enables identification at critical stages in the project preparation process to determine whether a project is expected to deliver sufficient benefits to continue expending resources on preparing and implementing it, often described as enabling projects to "fail fast."

---

[17] F. Gonguet et al. 2021. Climate-Sensitive Management of Public Finances—"Green PFM." IMF Staff Climate Note 2021/002. Washington, DC: International Monetary Fund.

[18] Green procurement practices refer to the purchase of goods and services that cause minimal adverse environmental impact and integrate climate, social, and governance goals into the procurement and supply chain.

[19] G. Schwartz et al., eds. 2020. Well Spent: How Strong Infrastructure Governance Can End Waste in Public Investment. p. 15.

The general principles of good governance design apply equally to developing high quality climate-informed PIM processes. The design of any climate-informed PIM process must consider the aspects of governance in the following:

(i)   **Institutional capacity.** The right institutions are established with the right powers and responsibilities. Institutions need to equip themselves with the authority, expertise, and resources to develop and implement the policies and initiatives within their mandates.

(ii)   **Whole-of-government coordination.** Integrated processes are established to enable coordination and knowledge transfer between agencies that interface with each other. Climate change is a cross-cutting issue that requires cooperation and information sharing among government agencies. In particular, the finance ministry is essential for ensuring the fiscal sustainability of climate investments and integrating climate considerations in macroeconomic planning.[20] Integrated processes enable seamless coordination, knowledge exchange, and data sharing among agencies responsible for climate-related policies, public finance, and environmental protection. Such coordination enhances the effectiveness of climate actions and ensures a coherent approach to climate-informed public financial management.

(iii) **Standardized criteria for evaluating investment projects.** Evaluation processes involve appropriate and relevant considerations, weighted appropriately. When evaluating climate-related projects and policies, a comprehensive set of criteria will assess environmental, social, and economic impacts. This includes considerations of GHG emissions reduction, climate resilience, cost-effectiveness, and alignment with sustainable development goals. The proper weighting of these factors ensures that climate considerations are adequately reflected in the evaluation process and leads to informed decision-making. This should apply not only to projects funded by the budget but to all projects including climate investments funded by donors.

(iv)   **Transparency and accountability.** Processes need transparency and accountability to build public trust. Transparency and accountability are essential principles in climate-informed PFM and PIM. Openness in decision-making processes, budget allocations, and project selection fosters public trust and confidence in government actions. This transparency also enables stakeholders to monitor the implementation of climate-related initiatives and ensure that resources are effectively used to address climate challenges.

(v)   **Stakeholder participation.** The public and private sectors and civil society bear significant risks from climate change creating the need for transparency, accountability, and stakeholder engagement. Engaging stakeholders— including civil society organizations, private actors, and local communities— is crucial for successful climate action. Developing stakeholder engagement

---

[20]   For more on the role of finance ministries in driving climate investment, see The Coalition of Finance Ministers for Climate Action. 2023. Strengthening the Role of Ministries of Finance in Driving Climate Action: A Framework and Guide for Ministers and Ministries of Finance.

plans that ensure the right feedback is obtained at the right time from the right groups is critical throughout the PIM process by enabling the integration of diverse perspectives, expertise, and local knowledge. It promotes ownership of climate initiatives, strengthens alignment with societal needs, and increases the chances of achieving sustainable outcomes.

(vi) **Independent scrutiny.** Processes incorporating levels of independent scrutiny—such as external evaluations, audits, and third-party reviews including reviews by finance ministries to ensure fiscal sustainability—will play a vital role in assessing the effectiveness and efficiency of climate-related policies and projects. Incorporating independent oversight provides an objective assessment of the outcomes and impacts of climate investments, identifies potential risks, and ensures accountability in the management of public funds allocated for climate actions. Some countries that have strong project appraisal and selection institutions have developed gateway processes at critical stages of a project's development. The gateway process achieves additional scrutiny by requiring independent peer review of infrastructure projects and programs by a public agency separate from the agency designing, procuring, and implementing the project or by a panel of experts at key points in the project life cycle.[21]

(vii) **Consistency and predictability**. Ensuring consistent application of rules and procedures is essential to avoid arbitrariness and promote fairness in climate-informed PIM. Consistency enables equitable access to resources by applying the same rules to all project stakeholders. It ensures that similar climate-related projects and policies are treated objectively and fairly, regardless of their location or sponsoring entity. It also provides clarity to stakeholders, improving predictability and enhancing trust in the system.

Greening Public Investment Management – Climate Fiscal Risk Analysis and Investment Planning

Countries can address the challenges identified for the climate-informed PIM climate by bringing adaptation and mitigation responsibilities closer to "business as usual" (BAU) investment planning. This involves investing in deep sector understanding of climate change risks, utilizing frameworks to identify projects and programs required that respond to high degrees of uncertainty, increasing the use of rolling investment plans, using inclusive planning processes, undertaking structured risk allocation, and establishing or enhancing approval gateways with climate risk expertise. The separation of responsibilities between BAU investment planning by line ministries and nationally determined contribution (NDC) and/or national adaptation plan (NAP) planning by other centralized agencies weakens coordination

---

[21] For further reading, see ADB. 2023. Gateway Framework: A Governance Approach for Infrastructure Investment Sustainability.

and inhibits the development of integrated, cohesive investment plans. Countries should analyze the institutional structures they have created, and review whether functions are separated in a way that reduces such coordination.

Typical country institutional responses to climate change have exacerbated coordination weaknesses in existing PIM and PFM systems. The scientific evidence base on climate change impacts country-by-country has often been created outside the line ministries that are responsible for BAU planning, and without deep ongoing involvement of line ministries. This is not surprising given the need for specialized expertise, the driving role that nongovernment institutions and donors have played in developing the scientific evidence base, and the capacity limitations within line ministries already struggling to close the investment gap. National institutions have typically been established to respond to this top-down, externally produced, and evolving evidence base, translating it into NDCs and NAPs. There is a similarity between how climate change planning has evolved, and the way public–private partnership (PPP) institutions evolved early on. In response to the possible benefits of PPPs, many countries established separate PPP institutional processes, including PPP laws, PPP procurement processes, and PPP centers to deploy PPPs separately from BAU planning. By creating a "two-track" process, the risk arose that PPP projects were not subjected to the same level or type of review as purely public projects. All projects must be subject to value for money analysis to ensure they deliver superior overall benefits in line with national policy priorities.

Coordination weaknesses often create two parallel investment planning processes: one for BAU line ministry planning, and another for climate change mitigation and adaptation. Lack of coordination between parallel processes make it even more challenging for climate change projects to translate NAPs into deployed investment. Adaptation and mitigation projects are identified separately from BAU planning, where the two need to be developed in concert. Adaptation and mitigation plans are not going through the same rigors of planning, allocation, and implementation as BAU planning, reducing their ability to be implementable. Separate climate change institutions are not well integrated fiscally with PFM processes, so funding is not allocated in the same way as for other projects. City climate-informed investment planning can be undertaken in a way that ensures that adaptation and mitigation planning occurs within the context of BAU investment planning (Box 1).

Investing in a Deep Sector Understanding of Climate Change

Climate data is available on national climate change impacts while localized sectors tend to lack adequate climate data for decision-making. Climate change risks arise not solely through the impact of climate change on the country's natural and climatic conditions, but through the interaction with current and future human settlement patterns. Even within each country, regional impacts can vary significantly. In addition, as settlement patterns and public needs evolve and grow—and

Box 1: Rapid City Appraisals in Six Pilot Asian Cities

The rapid city appraisal (RCA) planning methodology was developed under ADB technical assistance to enable cities to assess their current and future urban infrastructure needs until 2030 and identify and prioritize low-carbon and climate-resilient infrastructure projects. The RCA involves using downscaled climate data and greenhouse gas emissions to inform city decision-making on infrastructure investment and project prioritization. The ways in which the RCA methodology has been developed incorporate best practice governance approaches to climate-informed investment planning, including bringing together adaptation and mitigation planning with BAU planning.

The RCA includes four steps to develop a prioritized list of low-carbon and climate-resilient projects:

(i) Collect data on current and future planned service needs.
(ii) Appraise current and planned service needs in climate context to identify projects.
(iii) Prioritize adaptation and mitigation projects using multi-criteria analysis.
(iv) Undertake high-level project costing analysis.

The methodology also includes a climate vulnerability and emissions assessment. The methodology focuses on using publicly available data, as well as leveraging stakeholder knowledge through in-city workshops to efficiently obtain information and insights.

High-level RCAs were undertaken for Dhaka, Mandalay, Suva, Tbilisi, and Ulaanbaatar, and a more detailed RCA was undertaken for Ho Chi Minh City (in this case along with a high-level cost–benefit analysis of infrastructure options). The outputs of the Ho Chi Minh City RCA included

(i) 20 prioritized adaptation options from 49 concept options identified, and
(ii) 19 prioritized mitigation options from 40 concept options identified.

BAU = business as usual, RCA = rapid city appraisal.

Source: ADB, Ramboll, and Environ. Financing Low-Carbon, Climate Resilient Urban Infrastructure in Asia and the Pacific: Rapid City Appraisal Methodology – Six Pilot Cities. Unpublished.

infrastructure ages—investment is always ongoing. Policy action cannot be targeted at the level of "changes in increased mean precipitation." It is only based on specific sector risks in the context of other sector dynamics, investment plans, and infrastructure needs that policy action can be taken. Given that climate change research is still evolving, it is not surprising that the least is known about specific sector impacts, especially at the local level. Many countries find themselves in the position where they have a strengthening evidence base on national impacts such as average precipitation change, but this degrades at the regional and local levels, with limited detailed understanding at the local sector impact level on net impacts, risks, and needs (Figure 2).

One approach that may yield local efficiency benefits is for each sector to undertake a risk mapping exercise to identify the most critical areas. This can be done sector by sector. For mitigation, sector analysis should identify the highest emissions sectors and analyze the key sources of emissions within them. For adaptation, sector analysis should systematically work through the climate change impacts identified and through techniques such as developing red–amber–green heatmaps (Figure 3).

Figure 2: Climate Change Evidence Base Degradation Cascade

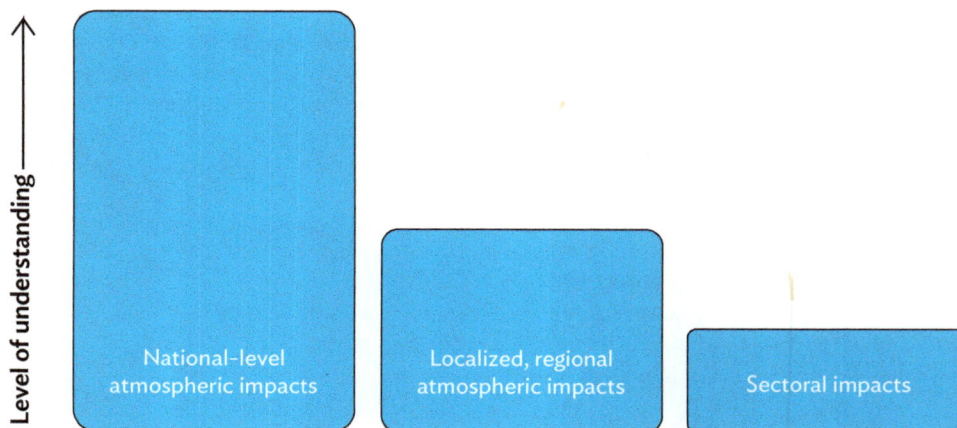

Source: Authors.

Figure 3: Transport Sector Adaptation Heatmap for Ho Chi Minh City

Climate Variables				Infrastructure at Risk			
Variables	Specific Risk	Rail/Metro/ Cable Car	Roads (incl. bridges)	Underground Infrastructure (tunnels, stations, etc.)	Airports (incl. runways)	Maritime Transport	Ports
Precipitation	Extreme Rainfall/ Flooding	🟧	🟧	🟧	🟧	🟩	🟨
	Changes in Mean Rainfall	🟨	🟨	🟨	🟨	🟨	🟨
	Drought	🟨	🟨	🟨	🟨	🟨	🟨
Temperature	Extreme Temperature	🟧	🟧	🟨	🟨	🟩	🟩
	Mean Temperatures Changes	🟨	🟨	🟩	🟩	🟩	🟩
Sea Level	Sea Level Rise	🟧	🟧	🟧	🟧	🟩	🟧
	Storm Surge	🟧	🟧	🟧	🟧	🟧	🟧
	Lightning and Storms	🟧	🟧	🟨	🟧	🟨	🟨
	Wind Speed	🟧	🟧	🟩	🟧	🟧	🟧
Humidity	Humidity	🟩	🟩	🟩	🟩	🟩	🟩
Other	Bushfires	🟨	🟨	🟩	🟨	🟩	🟩
	Interdependencies	🟨	🟨	🟨	🟨	🟨	🟨

🟧 Likely high level risk, needs consideration   🟨 Potential risk, needs investigation   🟩 Not a likely issue

Source: ADB. Financing Low-Carbon, Climate Resilient Urban Infrastructure in Asia and the Pacific: City Climate Investment Profile – Ho Chi Minh City. Unpublished.

By first identifying the areas of greatest impact, countries can ensure that scarce public resources are focused first on the areas of largest risk and greatest benefit. Having identified the areas of greatest impact, focused planning processes can then identify and develop integrated, cohesive responses that respond to climate change risks as part of improving services. This also reduces the risk of investment plans containing projects or initiatives that are undermined by climate impacts that were not properly identified. For example, investing in an irrigation system where the anticipated water source will no longer be viable. Once projects and programs are identified, they should then feed into sector investment plans, which are then approved as part of the budgetary process such that funds are allocated and fully funded and therefore able to progress to sustainable implementation.

Figure 4: Seven Cascading Uncertainties in Climate Change Investment Planning

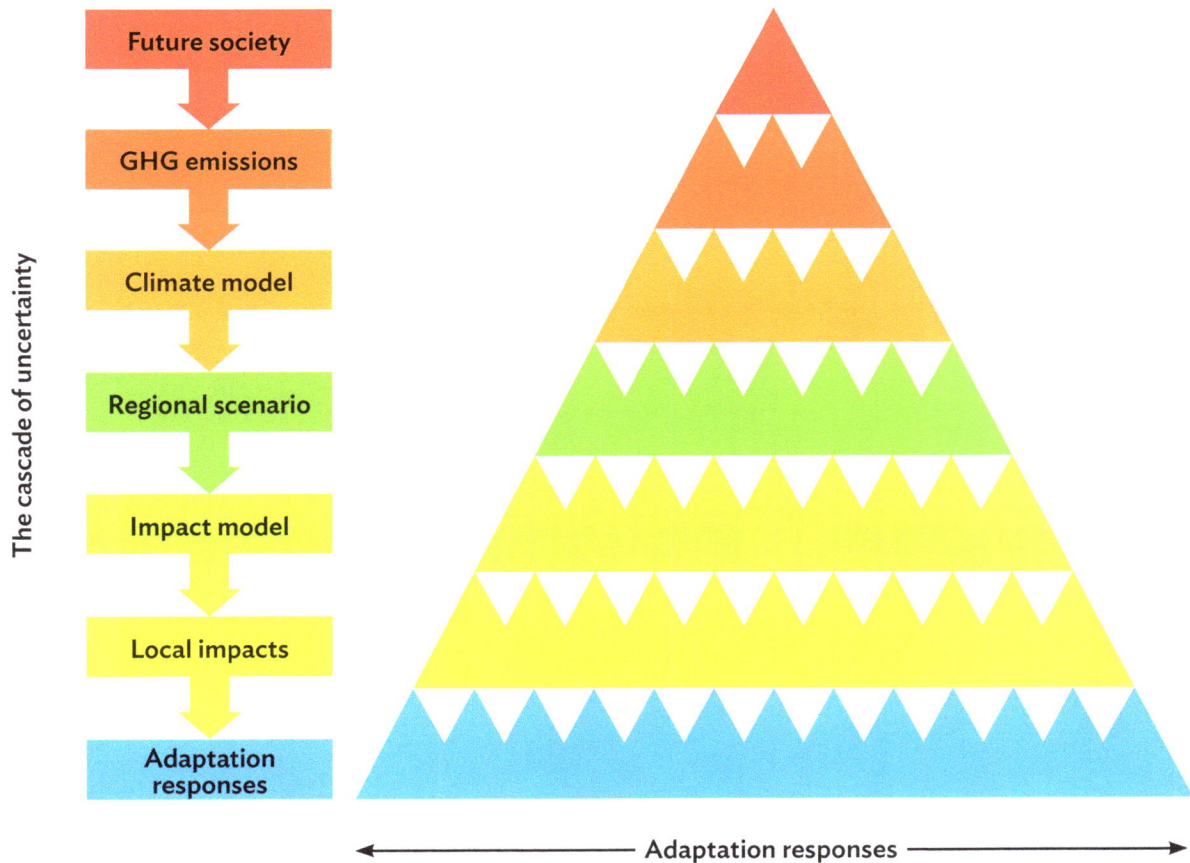

The cascade of uncertainty

Future society
GHG emissions
Climate model
Regional scenario
Impact model
Local impacts
Adaptation responses

Adaptation responses

Source: R. L. Wilby and S. Dessai. 2010. Robust Adaptation to Climate Change. *Weather*. 65 (7). pp. 180–185.

The evolving nature and depth of climate change knowledge and the range of possible global GHG emissions trajectories create high levels of uncertainty in country-specific and sector-specific impacts. For example, in Indonesia's agriculture sector, one Bappenas (the Government of Indonesia National Development Planning Agency) study found that rice production in certain provinces would decrease by more than 25.0%, whereas another study found that rice production in the same provinces would only decrease by 2.0%. How do line ministries develop investment plans in the face of such significant uncertainty? There are cascading types of uncertainty to which policymakers and planners must respond in planning under climate change (Figure 4). The cascade illustrates that uncertainty at each layer from the top downward compounds the level of uncertainty experienced at the level below. While uncertainty is a feature of all investment planning, climate variability is significantly greater than that typically observed in BAU planning. This heightens the difficulty in determining the appropriate response.

Country policymakers need to consider how to determine actions based on risk levels and decision dynamics. Watkiss, Cimato, and Hunt[22] consider identifying whether—in response to a specific sector risk—one of three types of urgent action is justified (Figure 5). Where current risks are high, then adaptation investment can be considered low or no-regret investment, and should be considered urgent. That is, in situations where the degree of risk is sufficiently high that on any standard project evaluation framework, the expected cost of the risk would justify investment

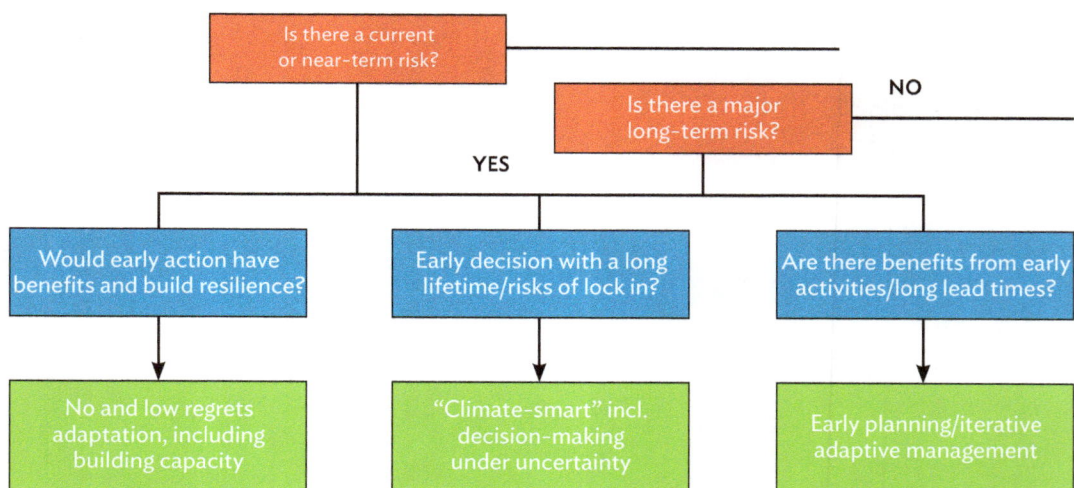

Figure 5: Framework for Adaptation Planning under Uncertainty

Source: P. Watkiss, F. Cimato, and A. Hunt. 2021. Monetary Valuation of Risks and Opportunities in CCRA3. Supplementary Report for UK Climate Change Risk Assessment 3 prepared for the Climate Change Committee. London.

---

22   P. Watkiss, F. Cimato, and A. Hunt. 2021. *Monetary Valuation of Risks and Opportunities in CCRA3.* Supplementary Report for UK Climate Change Risk Assessment 3 prepared for the Climate Change Committee. London.

to mitigate it. A no-regret investment would be made in the absence of any climate impact. Where decisions have a long lifetime—such as infrastructure—climate-smart design should predict adaptation risks. Where there are difficult-to-predict future risks and investment in preparation activities—including the planning, collection, and monitoring of data—countries should consider an iterative approach to respond effectively as more is known.

The process of identifying key climate changes and their sector impacts is not a one-off static process. Much like all investment planning, it is a continuous, rolling process to improve the responsiveness to changing climate impacts. Countries can benefit from embedding within their PFM frameworks the updating of investment plans to consider new information and understanding. Similar to adaptive learning and management used within adaptation planning, investment planning should not be seen as a static exercise. Rather, consider a process of rolling updates to investment plans, with a time horizon such as a 5-year investment plan with rolling annual updates. All sectors interact with others, so a single sector investment plan will inevitably depend on interactions with other sectors and the various institutions involved in planning for those interacting sectors.

Allocating risks of climate change between the public and private sector

Before identifying the projects and programs that the government will fund, countries should undertake risk allocation to carefully define the risks the public will bear. Planning, project, and program evaluation frameworks must evolve given that newly emerging adaptation risks of climate change are being allocated between the public and private sector, both deliberately and by default. As adaptation risks emerge (such as increased drought risk in the agriculture sector), they will be borne by default by some party, whether national or subnational government, businesses, or households. For example, increased drought risk for agriculture would be borne directly by farmers by default with reduced crop yields. Coastal inundation risk faced by coastal communities would be borne directly by those communities by default with property losses and repair costs, along with potential life loss. Each of these would then be expected to have second round impacts on the wider economy. However, national and subnational governments must determine the extent to which this default risk allocation is appropriate, or whether to devise policy mechanisms to transfer the risk elsewhere.

Since adaptation risks and potential losses can be large, there will be major economic and social ramifications for the way sector risks are allocated. In planning for BAU municipal stormwater recurring and capital expenditure, for example, decisions are being made on the extent to which the stormwater system should be upgraded to reduce the risk of settlements being flooded. Investment planning needs to address risk allocation and risk mitigation, including in the evaluation criteria used to assess projects and programs. Allocating risk is a process of either affirming the appropriateness of how risks will be borne or developing policy mechanisms that will shift the burden of those risks to other potential risk owners either in whole or in part. Table 3 provides examples of costs based on risk allocation for agriculture adaptation investments between the public and private sectors. If it

Table 3: Agriculture Adaptation Investments: Indicative Distribution of Costs Between the Private and Public Sectors

Adaptation Subprogram	Public Sector	Private Sector
Water Storage	Dams and reservoirs	Farm irrigation systems
Irrigation	Primary and secondary irrigation system	Tertiary irrigation system
Flood Protection	Dikes and embankments	Insurance premiums for farm assets
Seed Improvement	Development of new seeds Training of farmers	Seed costs
Pest Control	Development of pesticides Training of farmers	Pest control cost
Agricultural Research and Extension Services	Development of new varieties Training of farmers	Seed costs

Source: Authors.

is determined by policy that certain risks are rightly allocated to households or firms, it follows that the costs of investments that reduce such risks should in general be borne by them through user fees, since they are the beneficiaries of such investments. Often the costs of managing the risk are shared if there is an economic justification for the public (taxpayers) to subsidize some portion of costs allocated to the private sector. In the case of seed improvement, the public may fund the development of new seeds and the training of farmers, whereas farmers may fund the seed costs themselves.

Countries should consider a range of principles when allocating sector climate risks. Factors to consider in allocating risk include the following:

(i)   **Ability to manage the risk**. Classic risk allocation theory emphasizes allocating risks to those best able to manage them.[23] That is, those with better information and/or the ability to act differently or exert influence on actions that will affect the risks' expected impact and/or probability of occurrence. For example, allocating the risk of ensuring that a bridge under a PPP arrangement is built to a tolerance to withstand projected climate impacts might be best allocated to the private operator. This would be on the basis that they have both the expertise in and control of the design and construction of the bridge. The ability to manage risk must also take into consideration the insights from behavioral economics which suggests that people struggle to make rational decisions in circumstances with long time horizons and uncertainty.[24]

---

[23]   See for example IMF. 2016. Analyzing and Managing Fiscal Risks – Best Practices.

[24]   Government of the UK, Department for Environment, Food and Rural Affairs. 2010. Adapting to Climate Change: Analysing the Role of Government. *Defra Evidence and Analysis Series*. See Section 2.3 The Role of Government. London.

(ii)   **Distributional outcomes of bearing the risk**. Outcomes that are considered inequitable can arise because of the unequal distribution of climate risk both geographically and by sector. This is particularly the case where unequally distributed climate risk exacerbates inequalities affecting the vulnerable low-income groups financially unable to bear the risk.

(iii) **Financial capacity to bear the risk**. In addition to questions of distributional inequality, allocating risk to those financially unable to bear it can nonetheless result in increased fiscal risk exposure for the national government. For example, leaving farmers to bear the full impact of crop damage and reduced crop yields because of climate impacts such as flooding would be expected to reduce GDP and increase fiscal pressure on public budgets such as the need to subsidize food imports or provide emergency support to farmers.

(iv)   **Impact on incentives of bearing the risk**. Where a party does not bear risks that they can influence through their actions, that party might be incentivized to act in a way that fails to efficiently manage risk or even increases the level of risk. If there are no significant penalties or fines for excessive carbon emissions, companies may not have a strong incentive to reduce their GHG emissions and contribute to climate change mitigation. Governments providing substantial subsidies to fossil fuel companies can discourage the transition to renewable energy sources and maintain reliance on carbon-intensive fuels, exacerbating climate change.

Greening Public Investment Management – Project Appraisal

Strengthening governance for climate-responsive public investment requires a particular focus on climate analysis in project appraisal and selection. The International Monetary Fund (IMF) has developed the Public Investment Efficiency Index, which estimates the relationship between a country's public capital stock and indicators of access to and the quality of infrastructure assets. It refers to the difference between the expected or desired outcomes of public investments and the actual outcomes achieved. In other words, it assesses how well public funds are utilized to achieve the intended objectives, such as promoting economic growth, infrastructure development, or poverty reduction. The index has been applied in more than 100 countries The average efficiency gap for the Asia and Pacific region is 32.0%.[25] The significance of investment efficiency cannot be overstated, especially for fiscally constrained governments. Selecting the most economically efficient adaptation projects can have large economic benefits. Estimates of cost–benefit ratios for adaptation projects range from 2:1 up to 10:1.[26] Investing $1.8 trillion globally in five areas during 2020–2030 could generate $7.1 trillion in total net benefits. In other words, failing to seize the economic benefits of climate adaptation with

---

[25]   IMF. 2015. Making Public Investment More Efficient. Policy Paper.
[26]   Global Commission on Adaptation. 2019. Adapt Now: A Global Call for Leadership on Climate Resilience.

high-return investments would undermine trillions of dollars in potential growth and prosperity. Countries need to prioritize which adaptation investments they undertake because not all climate sector risks can be eliminated, and some investments may not be economically beneficial or fiscally sustainable.

To enhance project appraisal and selection process climate responsiveness, governments need to ensure evaluation criteria enable proper costing and prioritization of climate projects. Business case development—in which all the technical, legal, financial, and economic issues are assessed—is critical to ensuring the *right projects* get prioritized and implemented. Economic appraisal—applying cost-benefit analysis methodology—is a cornerstone of business case development and remains the gold standard for assessing the economic costs and benefits of climate action, and hence the use of limited public resources. Cost-benefit analysis is a well-developed methodological approach to assessing the economic costs and benefits of projects relative to a baseline. However, its application to climate action is less developed, and careful thought needs to be given to the quantification of the costs and benefits of climate action.[27] Specifically, countries must ensure that the following three cost types are incorporated in the evaluation of all projects and programs:

(i)   **Cost impacts of climate hazards on a project**. This includes the direct and indirect losses resulting from operational disruptions, which may include structural damage. It is essential to assess the cost of recovering from such disruptions and factor in the probability and timing of their occurrence.

(ii) **Costs of implementing climate mitigation options and adaptation measures**. This involves considering the expenses associated with developing structural capital works that protect against climate hazards.

(iii) **Indirect costs or externalities associated with operational disruptions caused by climate hazards**. These costs could include disruptions to businesses because of road closures arising from flooding or suspension of industrial production resulting from power shortages caused by extreme weather events. The expected value of these costs should reflect the impact and probability of occurrence throughout the project's life span.

Economic analysis of infrastructure investments should also include the identification and quantification of the associated benefits resulting from climate mitigation and adaptation features. These benefits can go beyond the project or program's original objectives and include risk reduction resulting from climate-related measures such as reduction in GHG emissions. In many respects, this mirrors the first and third cost categories: the benefit associated with avoided losses arising from investments that mitigate or adapt to climate hazards. The economic analysis should evaluate socioenvironmental co-benefits such as the protection of ecosystems, avoidance of travel disruptions and their costs, increased land value, and the safety of users by avoiding power shortages. It should also assess socioeconomic benefits such as impact on food security, health, human settlements, and poverty. These benefits may occur throughout the investment life cycle including the decommissioning phase, rather than solely during the period of operations. Other benefits can

---

27   World Bank. 2022. Climate Toolkits for Infrastructure PPPs. Washington, DC.

include increased operating life span and increased residual project value because of resilience to withstand climate hazards. Incorporating climate mitigation and adaptation into economic analysis can also increase potential access by developing countries to climate financing sources with lower financing costs. Calculating costs and benefits from mitigation investments is typically more straightforward as it requires only a carbon price to determine benefits, while adaptation investments require an estimate of climate-related losses avoided.

Existing investment planning should embed mitigation and adaptation processes to create a new "business as usual" and avoid creating separate processes. Armenia is an example of a country that updated its public investment management framework to take account of climate change and disaster risk and management (Box 2). Countries should develop a method of determining the extent of funding available for climate mitigation and adaptation. Mitigation and adaptation investments must be funded from the same scarce fiscal capacity as both BAU operations and existing sector investment planning. This can either be

---

Box 2: Armenia – Greening Public Investment Management

Armenia's PIM Decree, issued in October 2021, prescribes the process for evaluating and determining the priority of public investment projects with projected costs greater than AMD1 billion (about $2.6 million) and rising to AMD3 billion ($7.7 million) in 2024, including the use of multi-criteria analysis.[a] Projects below this threshold size utilize the general budgeting framework—which does not require multi-criteria project appraisal—and financing is approved based on the budget. All projects that need to go through a PIM Decree process require Investment Committee (headed by the Prime Minister, and including key ministers and one independent, nonvoting expert) approval before they can be included in the MTEF and annual budget.

The six evaluation criteria of public investment projects are:

(i)   The impact on human capital;
(ii) The public importance of the infrastructure, including urgency and necessity;
(iii) The extent of compliance with the strategy;
(iv) The impact of the project on climate change;
(v)   The project risk, including exposure to climate and disaster risks and risk management approach; and
(vi) The economic internal rate of return.

It is important to note that the original decree did not include Criteria 4 or Criteria 5 in terms of exposure to climate and disaster risks. The Decree was amended to consider both whether the investment facilitates adaptation to—or mitigation of—climate change, or if it is designed with climate proofing in mind. Guidance materials that provide methodologies for including these elements in investment appraisal are under development.

$ = United States dollars, AMD = Armenian dram, MTEF = medium-term expenditure framework, PIM = public investment management.

[a]   Decree N 472-L of the Prime Minister of the Republic of Armenia of 29 October 2021 on approving the procedure for identifying, developing, evaluating public investment programs, compiling and determining the list of priorities, approving the methodology for evaluating public investment programs and the model form of developing and evaluating the draft public investment programs in the Republic of Armenia.

Source: Authors.

through prescribing mitigation and adaptation funding that is determined to be fiscally sustainable—which is then allocated in rank order—or having mitigation and adaptation investments compete for the same funding pool as other investments and ultimately be prioritized in the same list as all other projects.

Economic appraisal should assess options for reducing climate risk. This includes risk reduction through mitigation or adaptation investment, transferring risk via contract (e.g., insurance), and retaining and provisioning for residual risk that is not reduced or transferred. There is no singular approach to determining where to use each option. Countries can consider three key criteria in developing policy options for a fit-for-purpose approach.[28] These are the evidence base to determine the best strategic option for assessing risks based on a climate impact assessment, the degree of efficiency to reduce costs without hindering investment outputs and quality, and the adaptability of investment to new and evolving climate-related risks.

Countries can—in some cases—transfer the risk of losses to a third party via contract, for example, an insurance contract. In economic terms, this is similar to adaptation investment since both cases involve paying a sum of money to reduce risk exposure. The difference with risk transfer is that the risk exposure is potentially more certain as it is written into a contract, although it also involves taking on counterparty credit risk such as the risk of the insurer's ability to pay out on the contract if called upon. The use of such financial instruments is highly dependent on the market in terms of availability and the willingness of a credible counterparty to take on the risk. The use of such instruments is also affected by the terms, particularly the risk premium that must be paid and the strictness of conditions that must be satisfied to be eligible for payout. Most forms of risk transfer can be expensive to hold and are typically most appropriate for low probability and very high-cost risks. The availability and relative attractiveness of transferring risk via financial instruments in the future will depend significantly on how the market evolves, both in terms of the products available especially in developing countries, and the pricing. Countries should frequently reassess the state of the market to determine when risk transfer is beneficial.

When risks are not reduced via adaptation investment or transferred via contract such as insurance, countries must decide the extent to provision for risk. Countries need to determine the sizes and nature of the residual climate risks within which they may want to make some allowance. This should include risks that the national government has allocated away since such risk allocation may not always work as intended with the risk ultimately being borne by the government. In this case, the government should have a strategy for financing and funding the costs arising from those risks as and when they occur. This is particularly the case given the diversity of probability distributions for different risks, including relatively predictable annual costs such as the cost of seasonal flooding becoming more severe and low-probability and high-cost events such as the cost of increased severity of 1-in-100-year extreme weather events like storms. Without provisioning, countries would need to finance and fund the cost of adaptation as and when risks occur. This

---

28   ADB. 2023. Climate Resilient Fiscal Planning: A Review of Global Good Practices. Manila.

can pose a significant disruption to the budget process and budgetary certainty and involves exposure to the state of international financial markets at the time financing is required, which may be uncertain. Countries can benefit from determining some level of provisioning to undertake, for example, capitalizing contingency funds. Determining the extent of provisioning to undertake involves policy considerations and trade-offs with other government priorities. Countries should consider the level of fiscal surplus available for allocation to the contingency fund, the level of statistical confidence in the expected cost for which the government is willing to assume the risk, and scenario analysis of combinations of climate events that are either linked or may occur at the same time.

Greening Public Investment Management – Funding, Financing, and Delivery of Priority Investments

After identifying the costs and risks of priority investments, the focus turns to the effective management of climate-related investments. This includes the allocation of funding to projects and programs within the cyclical budgeting process, financing and delivery, and post-implementation portfolio management. Best practice PFM involves the allocation of budget to the projects and programs selected and the integration of the investment planning process with the budgeting process. This ensures that projects and programs only proceed to implementation where they are fully funded within the country's fiscal constraints. Ensuring that projects and programs are fully funded before they are financed is a requirement of all BAU planning as well as climate-related investment.

Green investments—as with all investments—need to be fully funded before they can be financed. Funding refers to how the cost of investments will be paid for. The costs of the investment—including the present value of the initial capital cost, future operating costs, and the costs of finance—must be covered by payments from users or the government or a combination of these two payment sources. An investment where this is true is said to be fully funded. Many climate investments require direct public funding given they provide a public good, and user charges alone will not recover the costs of implementing the investment. As a result, the public sector will have to cover these costs in part or whole. Such investments—while not generating a financial return—could have a positive multiplier effect on the wider economy and cause increases in GDP that justify public investment.

Financing refers to the need to deal with the mismatch in timing between upfront development costs and future revenues. Finance can consist of either debt or equity. What makes finance different from funding is that it must be repaid. If an investment is fully funded, then it can be financed. This is because a fully funded investment generates cash flows that are enough to pay equity investors and debt providers their desired risk-adjusted returns. Conversely, if an investment project is not fully funded, then it cannot be financed. Funding sources should optimize the benefits to users, with public funding compensating for the shortfall between what a government can realistically charge users and the actual costs of construction, operation, and maintenance of the investment. These costs include payments for principal and interest, that is, servicing the debt. Even where financing is provided on a grant basis—such as the Green Climate Fund which provides about 41.0% of its portfolio in the form of grant financing—recipients are expected to make co-contributions, and the proposed investments are subject to the same criteria for loan financing. The key lesson is that countries must properly consider the fiscal and policy implications of financing their climate adaptation and mitigation investments alongside their other fiscal commitments.

With heightened competition for scarce public funding, reform will be needed to improve the efficiency of both revenue and expenditure to fund climate investments. Public sector financing for climate investments is constrained by levels of public debt, which in many DMCs are high or close to sustainable limits, due primarily to the extraordinary levels of support provided in response to the COVID-19 pandemic. While many government balance sheets have begun to bounce back, many of them have competing claims on scarce government resources, and reprioritization will have to take place to accommodate additional funding for climate action. Reforms will need to consider both the revenue and expenditure side of public finance resourcing. It is tempting for governments to simply raise revenue through increased taxes to fund new investment requirements, but it is often not economically efficient to do so if countries are constrained by institutional weakness in enforcing tax compliance. Cutting expenditure in other areas must be carefully considered to avoid a negative impact on vulnerable populations and the SDGs. The ADB 2022 Asian Development Outlook explicitly looks at this issue, suggesting that "Significant opportunities exist to expand the use of tax and other fiscal instruments to tackle environmental and health priorities while raising revenue. Fundamental tax reform to mobilize revenue better can be achieved and it is best done in tandem with efforts to strengthen tax administration and improve taxpayer morale."[29] The Asian Development Outlook update notes that there is potential across the region to increase tax revenue from a pre-pandemic average of about 16.0% of GDP by 3–4 percentage points.

Opportunities to strengthen revenue such as a carbon tax will depend on economy-specific circumstances including institutional capacity. A carbon tax can enable the shift toward clean energy and reduce carbon emissions. It allows countries to achieve their climate targets—as stated in their NDCs—cost-effectively and encourages them to increase their climate ambitions. The 2021 *ADB Energy Policy* recognizes the potential of well-designed and implemented carbon pricing mechanisms to drive the transition to cleaner energy sources. These mechanisms can accelerate the adoption of advanced low-carbon technologies, promote the use of renewable energy, facilitate the growth of e-mobility, encourage the switch to cleaner

29   ADB. 2022. *Asian Development Outlook (ADO) 2022: Mobilizing Taxes for Development.* Manila.

fuels, and promote the use of nonfossil fuel energy. The global interest in carbon pricing is growing, with about 68 countries already implementing either a carbon tax or an emissions trading system as of 2022.[30]

The private sector will need to play a role in both direct adaptation and financing as part of the efforts to mitigate and adapt to climate change. A range of additional external financing sources are available for climate-related investments. According to the ADB publication, *Accelerating Private Sector Engagement in Adaptation in Asia and the Pacific*, the private sector has an important role to play in climate adaptation. To protect their commercial interests in dealing with a changing climate, businesses in the private sector need to become "adaptors." The private sector is expected to act as "solution providers," supplying the technologies, services, and products required to adapt to the wide variety of physical climate risks that will impact communities, economies, and the environment. For the public sector to overcome fiscal constraints and bridge the considerable gap in financing requirements for investment in adaptation, the private sector will need to invest. Governments can utilize innovative forms of private sector financing—such as the issuance of green bonds—and blended finance may increase the volume of investment that can be undertaken sooner and may reduce the cost of such financing. PPPs and securitization of infrastructure assets can also provide additional financing opportunities.[31] Several countries have taken advantage of favorable terms available for buyers of green and related bonds. The Government of Indonesia's Ministry of Finance encourages the implementation of innovative public finance to enhance fiscal capacity and finance climate action, including Green Bond/*Sukuk* issuances and SDGs Indonesia One (Box 3).

PPPs have an important role to play in adapting to climate change, primarily because when PPP transactions are properly structured—with risks being allocated to the party best able to manage those risks at the lowest cost—they can provide considerable value for money to governments. Properly organized PPPs can enhance efficiency, but they also expose governments to various liabilities, including contingent ones. The uncertainty associated with infrastructure construction and operation—combined with the long-term contractual nature of PPPs—can result in significant fiscal risks. If PPPs are not carefully planned, designed, and managed, and if their fiscal treatment is insufficient, they can lead to considerable fiscal surprises.[32] Ultimately, all forms of investment (finance) must be paid for (funded) and therefore integrated with the budget whether climate-related or not.

The private sector has actively participated in various sectors to mitigate and adapt to climate change. For instance, private contractors are involved in constructing climate-resilient infrastructure, and private technology helps improve irrigation and early warning systems for water management. However, governments must create an enabling fiscal, institutional, and policy environment for the private

---

[30]   ADB. 2022. *Carbon Pricing for Energy Transition and Decarbonization.* Manila.
[31]   V. Rao. 2023. *Rethinking Infrastructure Financing for Southeast Asia in the Post-Pandemic Era.* Manila: ADB.
[32]   For a discussion of managing fiscal risks in PPPs and SOEs, see ADB. 2022. *An Infrastructure Governance Approach to Fiscal Management in State-Owned Enterprises and Public-Private Partnerships.* Manila.

Box 3: Indonesia – Green Financing – Issuance of Sukuk Bonds

The Ministry of Finance and PT. SMI—the state-owned financial institution entity charged with catalyzing and accelerating national infrastructure development in Indonesia—launched SDG Indonesia One (SIO) in 2018, an integrated platform to fund projects associated with the achievement of the Sustainable Development Goals (SDGs). SIO is a blended finance instrument designed to combine and channel public and private finance to the various stages of the project development life cycle. Public funds raised through this platform are expected to overcome the key financing barriers to SDG-related projects and to leverage large amounts of private sector investment. Total funds collected have reached $3.27 billion. The realization consists of 39 blended finance projects and 7 financing projects.

SOEs and SOE banks have issued several green bonds to finance climate and/or SDG activities. PLN—the state-owned power company—for example, issues green bonds to fund projects with clear environmental benefits to reduce GHGs. Social bonds are utilized for strategic projects directly impacting communities. Sustainability bonds can be exclusively applied to fund a combination of green and social projects. In May 2022, SOE bank—BNI—issued Green Bond I (Rp5 trillion/$334 million) for projects related to renewable energy, energy efficiency, waste, and waste to energy management, sustainable natural resources and land uses, biodiversity conservation, eco-friendly transportation, sustainable water and solid waste management, climate adaptation, green building, and sustainable agriculture.

In addition to green bonds, the government has successfully issued several green *Sukuk*, dating to the first issuance in 2018. Based on the *Sukuk* framework, climate adaptation (including disaster) is one of the eligible green projects, i.e., research leading to technology innovation with sustainability benefits, food security, flood mitigation, drought management, and public health management. In principle, the green *Sukuk* utilizes the results of the climate budget tagging mechanism and channels investment toward and across green sectors with the most climate change impact. Issuances and sector allocations are summarized below.

Green Sukuk Issuances

March 2018	Feb 2019	Nov 2019	June 2020	Nov 2020	June 2021	Nov 2021
1st Global Green Sukuk	2nd Global Green Sukuk	1st Retail Green Sukuk	3rd Global Green Sukuk	4th Global Green Sukuk	4th Global Green Sukuk	3rd Retail Green Sukuk
$1.25 billion	$750.00 million	Rp1.46 trillion ($104.40 million)	$750.00 million	Rp5.40 trillion ($385.70 million)	$750.00 million	Rp5.00 trillion ($346.00 million)

Cumulative Allocation of Global Green Sukuk by Sector

Sector	Allocation (%)
Energy efficiency	11
Renewable energy	5
Sustainable transport	41
Waste and waste to energy management	6
Resilience to CC for highly vulnerable areas and sectors/DRR	36

$ = United States dollars, BNI = Bank Negara Indonesia, CC = climate change, DRR = disaster risk recovery, GHG = greenhouse gas, PLN = Perusahaan Listrik Negara, PT. SMI = PT Sarana Multi Infrastruktur, Rp = Indonesian rupiah, Sukuk = Islamic Bond/Sharia-compliant bond.

Source: Authors.

sector to effectively adapt, provide solutions, and finance initiatives. To support private sector actors in making informed decisions, governments should supply critical data and information. Sector adaptation investment plans should clearly outline government institutional arrangements and objectives to guide private sector actors. As private investors typically have short-term horizons while climate risks manifest over the long term, public support in the form of financial incentives may be necessary to bridge gaps. Certain adaptation and mitigation projects may require budgetary allocation because of their "public good" characteristics.

Conclusion

The climate investment gap is an urgent challenge that requires immediate attention. While the urgent need to mitigate and adapt to climate change is widely accepted, investments in adaptation and mitigation projects remain insufficient. International consensus on the need for action has grown but concerted action needs to go beyond addressing climate change dynamics; it involves bridging infrastructure gaps faced by millions with green, inclusive, and resilient investments. As Asia and the Pacific experience frequent and severe climate-related disasters, it is critical to understand climate data and analyze risks in sectors like energy, transportation, water, sanitation, agriculture, and coastal areas to drive climate investment needs.

Strong governance within public financial management (PFM) and public investment management (PIM) processes are essential to effectively bridge the climate and infrastructure gap. Policymakers should avoid creating separate institutions, processes, and frameworks for climate-resilient infrastructure and instead should seek to integrate climate risk considerations into PFM and PIM frameworks. Nationally determined contributions (NDCs), national adaptation plans (NAPs), and sector adaptation plans (SAPs) should link to sector strategies, and fully integrate with PFM and PIM institutions and processes. This will help to ensure consistent planning and adherence to climate objectives. Where governance capacity is weak, improving PFM and PIM processes and the governance within them is critical to improving the quality of investment propositions.

The role of finance ministries is essential in coordination with environmental and other sector agencies as well as local jurisdictions where residents directly feel the impacts of climate change. Economic appraisal and selection of climate-responsive projects present significant opportunities to increase efficiency in utilizing scarce fiscal space. Finance ministries must play a central role in mainstreaming climate action within their core responsibilities of economic strategy, and fiscal and financial policy.

Public resources will not be sufficient to meet the need for resilient infrastructure investment. Private financing plays a valuable role as "solution providers" to supply the technologies, services, and products required to adapt to the wide variety of physical climate risks that will impact communities, economies, and the environment. For the public sector to overcome fiscal constraints and bridge the considerable gap in financing requirements for investment in adaptation, the private sector is also expected to function as "financiers" to provide market-based finance.

Ensuring adaptation and mitigation projects are fully funded in the budget cycle and throughout the project life cycle will contribute to unblocking the deployment of private sector financing and donor-provided climate finance. Strengthening governance for climate-responsive public investment requires a focus on climate analysis in project appraisal and selection, transparency, accountability, and stakeholder participation. Given the uncertainty over long-term climate impacts, rolling planning processes are needed to keep investment plans up to date with new climate information. Proper risk allocation—considering factors like risk management and financial and funding capacity—should be carried out to build a bankable and affordable pipeline of climate-resilient investment projects. Proper risk allocation also sends signals to the private sector as to which climate risks governments are willing to bear, and which will need to be managed by private firms and households.

Capacity development will continue to be essential to empower policymakers to identify and select high-quality and fiscally sustainable projects. Multilateral development banks play a role through technical assistance, lending, and grants to support policy reforms, capacity building, and leverage private financing to achieve climate goals. Innovative multilateral development bank financing mechanisms such as the ADB Innovative Finance Facility for Climate in Asia and the Pacific (IF-CAP) can leverage billions of dollars in climate change financing, and quality infrastructure governance contributes to a robust and sustainable pipeline of resilient infrastructure projects.

www.ingramcontent.com/pod-product-compliance
Lightning Source LLC
Chambersburg PA
CBHW050057220326

41599CB00045B/7447